A Guide to
AMERICAN STATES

Montana

THE TREASURE STATE

www.av2books.com

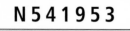

AV² provides enriched content that supplements and complements this book. Weigl's AV² books strive to create inspired learning and engage young minds in a total learning experience.

Your AV² Media Enhanced books come alive with...

Audio
Listen to sections of the book read aloud.

Key Words
Study vocabulary, and complete a matching word activity.

Video
Watch informative video clips.

Quizzes
Test your knowledge.

Embedded Weblinks
Gain additional information for research.

Slide Show
View images and captions, and prepare a presentation.

Go to **www.av2books.com**, and enter this book's unique code.

Try This!
Complete activities and hands-on experiments.

BOOK CODE

N 5 4 1 9 5 3

AV² **by Weigl** brings you media enhanced books that support active learning.

... and much, much more!

Published by AV² by Weigl
350 5th Avenue, 59th Floor
New York, NY 10118
Website: www.av2books.com   www.weigl.com

Library of Congress Cataloging-in-Publication Data

McLuskey, Krista, 1974-
 Montana / Krista McLuskey.
   p. cm. -- (A guide to American states)
 Includes index.
 ISBN 978-1-61690-798-3 (hardcover : alk. paper) -- ISBN 978-1-61690-474-6 (online)
 1. Montana--Juvenile literature. I. Title.
 F731.3.M383 2011
 978.6--dc23
                        2011018338

Printed in the United States of America in North Mankato, Minnesota

052011
WEP180511

Project Coordinator Jordan McGill
Art Director Terry Paulhus

Photo Credits
Every reasonable effort has been made to trace ownership and to obtain permission to reprint copyright material. The publishers would be pleased to have any errors or omissions brought to their attention so that they may be corrected in subsequent printings.

Weigl acknowledges Getty Images as its primary image supplier for this title.

Contents

The roots of Montana's rodeos go back to the Old West, when cowboys would hold competitions during cattle drives and roundups.

Introduction

When Meriwether Lewis and William Clark first explored Montana in the early 1800s, they were awestruck by the open plains and delighted by the wide range of animals that roamed the land. After reaching the Great Falls, which is on the Missouri River in what is now Montana, Lewis wrote in his journal that it was "the grandest sight" that he had "ever beheld."

Today much of the landscape that Lewis and Clark crossed remains unchanged. The dense forests, rugged mountains, and rushing rivers are still abundant with fish and other wildlife. The river canyons, mountain meadows, and Great Plains of Montana have earned the state the unofficial nickname of the "Last Best Place."

There are more than 22 million acres of forest in Montana.

Montana's Glacier National Park, part of the Waterton-Glacier International Peace Park, has more than 250 lakes.

Montana is one of the few states left without big-city noise, pollution, and crowds. Skyscrapers are scarce, and the population is relatively small. In fact, there are fewer people in the entire state than there are in many U.S. cities. Many Montanans live on ranches or farms, away from the fast pace of urban life.

A number of Montanans depend on the land for their livelihood, including farmers, ranchers, miners, and loggers. Many Montanans also cherish the land for what it offers in recreation. People who love the outdoors can hike, camp, fish, and ski in the natural beauty of the state. In fact, many people move to Montana to pursue outdoor activities, such as fly fishing, downhill skiing, and snowboarding. It is no coincidence that some members of the U.S. Snowboard Team live in Montana year-round.

Where Is Montana?

Montana is located in the northwestern United States. Though Lewis and Clark traveled many months to get there, Montana is easily reached in the modern era of interstate highways and airplanes. Still, people traveling by automobile are often surprised at the size of the state. The highways seem endless, stretching as far as the eye can see. The forests are immense. From the air, visitors have similar perceptions. The mountains, seen from overhead, are tremendous in scope.

The state's road conditions can change in a flash. It can be dry one moment and icy the next. In the winter interstates sometimes close due to heavy snow. However, air travel is now available throughout the state. International airports are located in Billings, Glacier Park, Glasgow, Great Falls, and Missoula. Many smaller airports dot the rest of state.

Ponderosa pines have soft wood, which Montanans use to make many items, such as fences and snowshoes. The roots are used to create blue dye.

With its high mountain peaks, forests, prairies, and valleys, the Montana landscape is beautiful and diverse. Wild rivers and other bodies of water crisscross the land and help define the state's regions. The Missouri River rises in the south and flows north and then east. The Yellowstone River flows from Wyoming through Yellowstone National Park and then north and east across Montana. The state's largest lake is Fort Peck Lake, which was made by humans. The largest natural lake is Flathead Lake.

A deep appreciation of the land has prompted many Montanans to protect the environment. To reduce automobile pollution, some cities offer free access to bikes. **Environmentalists** pursue ways to keep the water clean and the wilderness free from development.

I DIDN'T KNOW THAT!

The land area of Montana is 145,552 square miles.

Montana is the fourth-largest state in the nation. Only Alaska, Texas, and California are larger.

Montana's largest artificial lake covers 83 square miles. Fort Peck Lake was created when the Missouri River was dammed. The lake's shoreline is 1,520 miles long.

Logan Pass runs along the Continental Divide. Rivers on the east flow into the Gulf of Mexico and Atlantic Ocean. Rivers on the west flow into the Pacific Ocean.

Mapping Montana

Four other states border Montana. Idaho is to the west and south, and Wyoming is to the south. North Dakota and South Dakota are to the east. Three Canadian provinces lie to the north. They are British Columbia, Alberta, and Saskatchewan. Montana has two distinct land regions. The Great Plains are in the eastern part of the state, and the Rocky Mountains are in the western part.

Sites and Symbols

STATE SEAL
Montana

STATE BIRD
Western
Meadowlark

STATE FLOWER
Bitterroot

STATE FLAG
Montana

STATE ANIMAL
Grizzly Bear

STATE TREE
Ponderosa Pine

Nickname The Treasure State

Motto *Oro y plata*
(Gold and Silver)

Song "Montana," words by Charles Cohan
and music by Joseph E. Howard

Entered the Union November 8, 1889, as
the 41st state

Capital Helena

Population (2010 Census) 989,415
Ranked 44th state

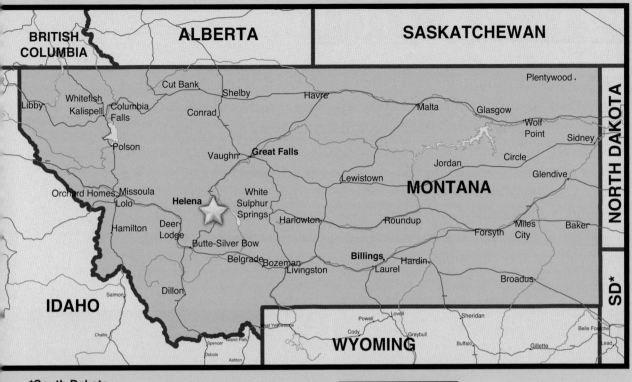

BRITISH COLUMBIA

ALBERTA

SASKATCHEWAN

NORTH DAKOTA

SD*

Libby
Whitefish
Kalispell
Columbia Falls
Cut Bank
Shelby
Conrad
Havre
Malta
Glasgow
Plentywood
Wolf Point
Sidney

Polson

Vaughn
Great Falls

Lewistown

MONTANA

Jordan
Circle
Glendive

Orchard Homes
Missoula
Lolo
Helena

White Sulphur Springs

Harlowton
Roundup
Forsyth
Miles City
Baker

Hamilton
Deer Lodge
Butte-Silver Bow
Belgrade
Bozeman
Livingston
Billings
Laurel
Hardin
Broadus

Dillon
Salmon

IDAHO

Challis
Spencer
Island Park
Dubois
Ashton

West Yellowstone
Powell
Lovell
Cody
Greybull
Buffalo

WYOMING

Sheridan
Belle Fourche
Gillette
Lead

*South Dakota

STATE CAPITAL

Helena, a city of about 30,000 people, is where the state legislature meets. The main part of the **capitol** was erected from 1899 to 1902. Two granite-faced wings were added in 1912. The original architects, Charles E. Bell and John H. Kent, relocated to Helena because the state legislature declared that the planners had to come from Montana. The dome that they designed is 165 feet high and is topped with a bronze statue of Lady Liberty.

LEGEND

— Road
— River
⭐ State Capital
• City
▭ Montana
— State Border

N

Map Scale

0   100 Miles

United States

Hawai'i   Alaska

Montana

9

The Land

The Rocky Mountains cover the western third of the state. More than 50 mountain ranges make up Montana's Rockies. Glaciers and rivers are found in the mountainous areas, too. Some of these rivers flow westward, toward the Kootenai and Clark Fork rivers. Others move eastward, to the Yellowstone and Missouri rivers.

The land is constantly changing but stays beautiful. Melting glaciers slowly move rocks and debris. Forest fires, often sparked by lightning, destroy many acres annually, yet the fires are followed by new growths of trees.

MISSOURI RIVER

The Missouri River is one of the longest rivers in the United States. It begins where the Gallatin, Madison, and Jefferson rivers meet in Montana. From there, it runs more than 2,300 miles, eventually flowing into the Mississippi River in Missouri.

GLACIER NATIONAL PARK

The state has 60 glaciers, which are ice masses that form in places where less snow and ice melts than accumulates. The glaciers move over time, usually a few inches per year, and most often downhill.

Lewis and Clark Caverns feature caves 300 feet below Earth's surface.

The state leads the nation in the training of smokejumpers. These firefighters parachute into remote areas that vehicles cannot reach. Once they reach the ground, smokejumpers tackle the flames at close range.

BLACKFOOT RIVER

Melting snow feeds Montana's 9,686 rivers and streams. Blackfoot River and many other waterways are considered recreation destinations.

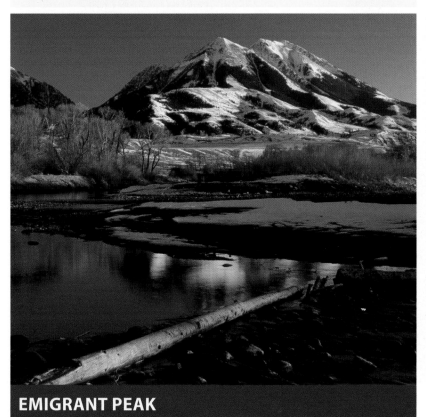

EMIGRANT PEAK

Montana has 3,328 summits, including Emigrant Peak, which overlooks Paradise Valley in the southwest part of the state.

Lake Shelburne is in the **chinook** zone of northwest Montana. When warm, moist air from the Pacific hits the Rockies, it rises. This causes precipitation in the mountains, which warms the air moving eastward. The chinook zone, where the lake sits, is on the eastern side of the mountains. The lake can overflow its banks when there are warm chinook winds.

Climate

Montana straddles the Continental Divide, a geographical line running through the Rocky Mountains from which water flows either east or west in the continental United States. In Montana, the tall mountains create two distinct climate regions. To the west of the mountains, the weather is milder. To the east, winters can be harsh. Average January temperatures range from 27° Fahrenheit in western Montana to 10° F in eastern Montana.

The state takes part in a network of National Heritage Programs, which track weather's effects on habitats and the species that are trying to survive. In Montana's wetlands, changes in weather and land use can dramatically affect what happens to plants and wildlife.

Average Annual Precipitation Across Montana

The amount of rainfall that different cities and towns in Montana typically receive each year can vary widely from place to place. What aspects of the geography of Montana do you think contribute to this variation?

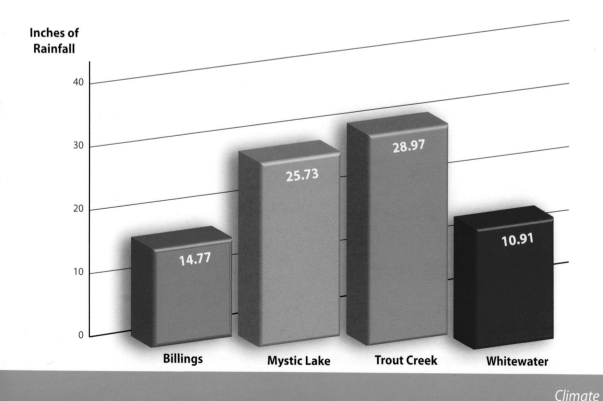

Inches of Rainfall

- Billings: 14.77
- Mystic Lake: 25.73
- Trout Creek: 28.97
- Whitewater: 10.91

Natural Resources

One-fourth of Montana is covered in thick forests. Douglas fir, spruce, pine, and cedar are very important to the state's economy. The trees are cut down to make products such as paper, pencils, and log homes. Many of the trees logged for commercial use in Montana are from the western part of the state.

In the northeast, in the valleys of the plains, and in other spots, the land is used for farming. Elsewhere, much of the land is used for raising livestock.

Kootenai National Forest is in northwestern Montana and reaches into the panhandle of northeastern Idaho. Logging is allowed in the federal forests but controlled by the U.S. Forest Service.

Kerr Dam generates hydroelectricity. Montana ranks among the top five states for hydroelectric power.

The Great Plains of eastern Montana were swampland millions of years ago. As plants and animals died, they sank to the bottom of the swamp. Their remains developed into coal, which has been an important resource. Montana also produces petroleum and natural gas, though production has been declining as reserves are used up. Today the state's mighty rivers produce hydroelectric power, and nearly one-third of the electricity in the state is generated by water power.

Early settlers were delighted to strike gold in Montana. Since then many other precious metals, such as copper and silver, have been discovered. In more recent years, Montana's economy has relied more heavily on another precious resource, however. The beauty of the land is being used to attract visitors.

Christmas trees are grown on tree farms in Montana. Each November and December the trees are shipped nationwide.

The extraction of metals has polluted the soil and water and harmed plant and animal life in parts of the state. In 1980, federal law began requiring mining operations to report releases of deadly chemicals and to clean up mining sites.

A mining site in the town of Anaconda poisoned the land with deadly chemicals. In 1994 the Anaconda mining area became a **Superfund** site. Montana was given U.S. government aid to restore the area.

Digital maps are being created of "environmentally sensitive" areas throughout the state. The hope is that national, state, and local agencies can use the maps as common ground when planning changes in land use.

Plants

The plants growing among Montana's peaks and valleys range from tall evergreen trees to grasses. The mountainous areas are covered with forests. However, at each level, from the mountaintops to the valleys, there are different, distinct collections of plant life.

The mountainsides are largely covered in towering spruce, pine, cedar, and Douglas fir trees. Wildflowers such as bluebells, asters, and brightly tinted Indian paintbrushes grow nearby. At the highest elevations, above the cone-producing trees on the mountains, there is a treeless area where alpine vegetation, such as dwarf willows, grows. Below the timber-covered mountainsides is the grassland of the valleys.

The plains are covered with mixed grasses. In the eastern plains spiky prairie cacti poke up among shoots of blue grama grass and needlegrass.

CHERRY TREES

Among the plants most often farmed in Montana are cherry trees. The most popular varieties grown include Lambert, Lapin, and Royal Anne.

DOUGLAS FIR

The most common type of tree found on Montana's mountains is the Douglas fir.

PONDEROSA PINE

American Indians often peeled the bark from ponderosa pines and ate the inner bark.

NODDING ONION

Early European settlers used the bulbs of nodding onion plants as flavoring in their cooking. American Indians used the plant's juice to treat colds.

American Indians used more than 50 kinds of Montana's local plants for medicine.

The Bitterroot Valley was named after the bitterroot, a plant whose roots were eaten by the American Indians. The root was often boiled and mixed with meat or berries.

The bitterroot flower is pinkish and blossoms in the spring. The plant is actually an herb.

Seven to nine million seedlings are planted each year in the state to replenish trees cut for timber.

Although they are now rare, grizzly bears inhabit the dense forests of Montana's Rocky Mountains. Grizzlies grow as tall as 8 feet and can weigh more than 1,000 pounds, yet they can move as fast as a horse. There are six national grizzly recovery zones, and three are in Montana. They are Cabinet-Yaak, Northern Continental Divide, and Yellowstone. In these areas, grizzly bears are protected, so that their numbers can increase.

Another rare animal, the bald eagle, soars in the Montana skies. After being hunted to near **extinction**, bald eagles have begun to return to the region. Moose, mountain goats, and elk also roam Montana, in the west. The grassy eastern plains are home to herds of pronghorn antelope and deer.

MOUNTAIN GOAT

The mountain goat is one of a kind in the world and occurs only in the U.S. Northwest. Domestic goats look like mountain goats but are not closely related.

GRIZZLY BEAR

The grizzly bear's blonde-tipped hair and its shoulder hump **distinguish** it from the black bear.

COUGAR

Cougars, which are hard to spot in the wild, are known as the Ghosts of the Rockies.

RING-NECKED PHEASANT

The ring-necked pheasant and hundreds of other bird species inhabit Montana.

Montana's rivers contain a "living fossil." The paddlefish, the state's largest fish, is about 5 feet in length and can weigh 100 pounds. The species has remained mostly unchanged for about 300 million years.

The wolf was hunted to near extinction because people fear wolves. Gray wolves were **reintroduced** to Yellowstone National Park in 1995 and 1996. Since then many pups have been born in the park.

Tourism

Montana's wide-open spaces, remote mountain pathways, and snow-covered slopes draw about 10 million tourists annually. Tourism employs tens of thousands of state residents. Visitors go skiing in winter. In summer, they go hiking or horseback riding or take in one of the state's many rodeos.

Yellowstone National Park, in the south, is a major tourist attraction. Yet another is on the northern border. There, Montana's Glacier National Park joined with Canada's Waterton National Park in 1932 to create the beautiful Waterton-Glacier International Peace Park. In addition, there are 43 state parks and numerous recreation areas and monuments to see and enjoy.

WATERTON-GLACIER INTERNATIONAL PEACE PARK

Waterton-Glacier International Peace Park has more than 700 miles of hiking trails.

YELLOWSTONE NATIONAL PARK

Yellowstone National Park lies mostly in Wyoming, but three of the park's entrances are located in southern Montana.

ROCKY MOUNTAINS

Nearly one-third of the land in Montana is publicly owned and administered by the federal or state government. The vast tracts of undeveloped land include most of the Rocky Mountains, which attract tourists who ski, hike, and climb the peaks.

MILES CITY

Miles City bears the nickname the Cowboy Capital of the World. The popular Miles City Bucking Horse Sale features rodeo events and live concerts.

The ski resorts in Montana are among the least crowded in the country, partly because of the state's low population.

Tourists spent almost $3 billion traveling through Montana in 2009.

Waterton-Glacier International Peace Park covers more than 1 million acres of land and has more than 60 species of mammals and more than 270 species of birds.

Industry

Montana has nearly three times as many cows as people. The 2.6 million Montana cows provide milk and beef. There are also about 250,000 sheep in the state. In addition to milk and meat, the sheep provide wool, which is spun into items such as sweaters and blankets. In addition, ostrich and emu farms have been increasing in number.

Industries in Montana
Value of Goods and Services in Millions of Dollars

Many of Montana's industries relate directly to the natural resources of the state, including agriculture and mining. Increasingly, however, people are employed in jobs in the service sector, which range from serving tourists to providing health care or performing government functions. Why might this be so?

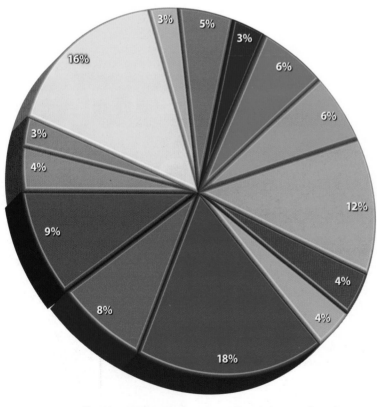

LEGEND

Agriculture, Forestry, and Fishing	$1,163
Mining	$1,667
Utilities	$1,054
Construction	$2,025
Manufacturing	$2,002
Wholesale and Retail Trade	$4,225
Transportation	$1,570
Media and Entertainment	$1,370
Finance, Insurance, and Real Estate	$6,347
Professional and Technical Services	$2,740
* Education	$164
Health Care	$3,359
Hotels and Restaurants	$1,281
Other Services	$1,061
Government	$5,926
TOTAL	**$35,954**

*Less than 1%. Percentages may not add to 100 because of rounding.

Almost 30,000 farms and 57.5 million acres of cropland cover Montana, which ranks among the top states in wheat production. Other crops grown in the state include barley, sugar beets, sunflowers, and mint.

Montana also has a large forestry industry. One of the state's great challenges has been finding a balance between logging, which employs many people, and protecting the land and its resources for future generations. More than two-thirds of the state's forests are open to logging.

The industries outside agriculture that employ the most residents involve trade, transportation, the utilities, or government work. Tourism is not far behind, as are health and education.

Both beef cows and dairy cows are raised in Montana, but beef cows are more numerous.

Goods and Services

In stores across the state, many products display a "Made in Montana" sticker. The Made in Montana program's main goal is to help Montanans succeed in business. Products crafted or grown and prepared in the state bear this seal. Buyers of these products know that they are helping to support local businesses.

From jams to gems, Montana produces a variety of quality goods. The state is famous for its juicy chokecherries, plums, and huckleberries, most enjoyed in jams, preserves, jellies, and syrups. Yogo sapphires from western Montana are crafted into fine jewelry. Copper bracelets, belt buckles, and cookware are all crafted in Montana.

Products with the label "Made in Montana" include honey. The state is also known for coffee, candy, and jams.

The production of high-tech goods is on the rise. Laser products used in dentistry, environmental cleanup, and underwater imaging are now an important part of Montana's manufacturing industry.

Montana's workforce is known for a high level of education. Despite its relatively sparse population, Montana has numerous schools of higher education. Many colleges and universities are sponsored by the state, including the University of Montana and Montana State University. Several colleges have technical schools, which offer specialized training in engineering and other fields. Many companies find the skilled and educated workers to be a good reason for setting up businesses in the state.

The service sector, however, has become the most important part of Montana's economy. It accounts for more than three-quarters of the state's economy. The many types of service employment include government jobs, jobs in finance, and hotel and restaurant positions.

Log homes manufactured in Montana are shipped as far away as Japan.

Some of Montana's high-technology industries are involved in the research and development of lasers.

Montana has two state gemstones, the agate and the sapphire. Sapphires of many colors are found in the state, but its cornflower blue sapphires are especially famous.

Jobs in the service sector are growing at a faster pace than jobs in manufacturing.

Many government workers have jobs related to taking care of parks and natural areas.

Hunting is a popular activity in the state. Some Montanans make their living as hunting guides.

Bitterroot Valley has numerous vegetable and fruit canneries.

American Indians

The American Indians who inhabited Montana can be divided into two regional groups. There were those who lived on the Great Plains in eastern Montana and those who lived in or near the Rocky Mountains. The Kootenai lived in the mountains, though extreme winter cold would force them down to the foothills every year. The Crow, Cheyenne, and Blackfoot lived on the Great Plains. They became known as Plains Indians.

The thousands of bison, also called buffalo, that thundered across the plains of Montana were important to the early inhabitants. Each part of the animal had a special use. The Plains Indians depended on bison as a food source. They smoked and dried some of the animals' meat to preserve it for future use. Hides and bones were used for clothing, blankets, **moccasins**, tools, and tepees. To catch the swift-moving animals, hunters built corrals near cliffs and drove stampeding herds into them. They chased the bison off the cliffs' edges, known as bison jumps, or *pishkun* in the Blackfoot language. The hunters then retrieved the bison carcasses from below.

American Indians hunted bison. The animals still thrive in Montana's grasslands. Their thick coats protect them from sun, wind, and snow.

The arrival of horses forever changed the way American Indians hunted. By 1750 most groups in the mountains and on the plains had horses. The hunters no longer had to wait for bison to enter the area. Instead, they could follow the bison on horseback and charge alongside their prey, killing at close range.

The availability of horses also changed relationships among American Indian groups. Beforehand, the groups rarely came into contact. Horses bridged the distance. While traveling, American Indians could carry more food, clothing, and other **necessities**. They could meet for **powwows** and other special events.

By the late 1700s bison hunting was much easier. American Indians no longer hunted bison just for survival. Products from the animals were also traded and sold.

The Crow and Blackfoot sometimes lured bison to the edge of a cliff by cloaking the hunters in animal skins.

The Absarokee was the original name for the Crow. Absarokee means "Children of the Large Beaked Bird" in the language of the Hidatsa people.

Montana's streams provided fish for American Indians. Today, Montana's American Indians have fishing rights on the reservations and beyond.

Evidence of a group of humans living in Montana between 9000 BC and 8000 BC has been found near Helena. This group is known as the Folsom.

Explorers and Missionaries

The United States paid about $15 million to France for the Louisiana Territory in 1803. This deal, known as the Louisiana Purchase, gave the United States a huge tract of land stretching from Louisiana in the south to Canada in the north. From east to west, the territory extended from the Mississippi River to the Rocky Mountains. The Louisiana Purchase doubled the size of the United States, and it made what is now Montana the property of the United States.

President Thomas Jefferson sent Meriwether Lewis and William Clark to explore the new area, beginning in 1804. They traveled up the Missouri River, reaching what is now Montana in 1805. Upon their return in 1806, Lewis and Clark reported that many fur-bearing animals, such as beavers, lived in the area. This news inspired the next set of explorers to visit Montana.

Chief among the newcomers were fur traders and trappers, known as mountain men. Fort Raman became Montana's first fur-trading post less than a year after Lewis and Clark's **expedition**. Then, in 1841, a Jesuit missionary named Father Pierre Jean de Smet founded St. Mary's Mission, the first permanent white settlement in the region.

In the 1870s, settlers in the Far West asked U.S. forces to move American Indians off the land. Nez Percé Chief Joseph led his people on a 1,400-mile retreat after battling to stay. They attempted to reach Canada but were forced to surrender to U.S. soldiers in Montana in 1877.

Timeline of Settlement

Early Exploration

1805 A French trader named Toussaint Charbonneau and his Shoshone wife, Sacagawea, help Lewis and Clark find their way through Montana.

1806 Upon their return to the East, Lewis and Clark talk about the natural wonders of the region that now includes Montana.

Traders and Travelers

1807–1840 Fur trappers and traders arrive. So many beavers are trapped that the animal almost becomes extinct in Montana.

First Settlements

1841 Father Pierre Jean de Smet establishes a mission about 25 miles south of today's Missoula. He brings the Christian religion and new methods of agriculture to the American Indians.

1852 A prospector finds gold at Gold Creek. Because of this and later gold strikes, additional settlers arrive.

Territory and Statehood

1863 Montana becomes part of the newly created Idaho Territory.

1864 President Abraham Lincoln creates the Montana Territory, using the Bitterroot Mountains as a divide between Montana and Idaho.

1866 Nelson Story reaches Montana with longhorn cattle driven up from Texas. This begins the ranching industry in the region.

1876 In the Battle of the Little Bighorn, American Indian warriors overcome the U.S. 7th Cavalry, led by George Armstrong Custer.

1880 The first railroad tracks are built in Montana. Railroads soon increase the number of settlers.

1889 Montana becomes the 41st state.

Early Settlers

Gold was discovered at Gold Creek in the 1850s, but the Montana gold rush began in earnest in 1862, when this precious metal was discovered along Grasshopper Creek. Hundreds of miners headed to Montana, to try to make their fortunes. Many miners then turned to raising cattle on the open ranges as well.

Map of Settlements and Resources in Early Montana

4 *In 1852, a trapper finds gold at Gold Creek. Other gold strikes follow. Prospectors stream in.*

1 *When Lewis and Clark arrive in 1805, they discover a wealth of fur-bearing animals. After news of their findings reaches the East, trappers head to what is now Montana.*

5 *In 1862, additional gold is found at Grasshopper Creek, the news gets out, and prospectors begin arriving from the East and from farther west.*

2 *In 1829, Fort Union is established by the American Fur Company on the Missouri River. Other forts soon follow.*

3 *St. Mary's Mission is the first permanent white settlement in Montana. It is started in 1841.*

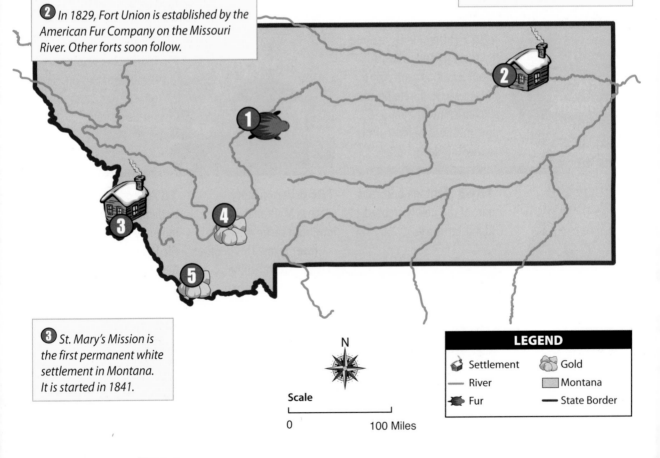

N

Scale

0   100 Miles

LEGEND		
Settlement		Gold
River		Montana
Fur		State Border

As prospectors and settlers began moving to Montana in large numbers, the U.S. government moved Montana's American Indians to **reservations**. Eventually, however, the white settlers were not content with that arrangement either. They also wanted the reservation land to farm and mine.

Some American Indian groups fought back in the Great Sioux War of 1876–1877, winning a historic battle near the Little Bighorn River in 1876. In that battle, Sioux and Cheyenne warriors, led by Sitting Bull, Crazy Horse, and other chiefs, fought and beat Lieutenant Colonel George Armstrong Custer and his soldiers. The fight became known as the Battle of the Little Bighorn. The hill on which much of the fighting took place, and on which Custer and more than 200 of his men were killed, became known as Last Stand Hill. However, by 1877, almost all of Montana's American Indians had been defeated.

Lieutenant Colonel George Armstrong Custer ignored orders to wait for reinforcements on the day he was defeated at the Battle of the Little Bighorn.

A bronze statue of Meriwether Lewis and William Clark stands in Great Falls.

The Battle of the Little Bighorn is considered to be one of the worst disasters suffered by the U.S. Army in its history.

Miners who were unlucky in the California gold rush tried mining in Montana. Last Chance Gulch, now Helena, was the location of one of the early gold strikes in the area.

A large vein of copper was discovered in Butte Hill in the late 1800s. It became known as the Richest Hill on Earth.

From 1863 to 1865, more than $30 million worth of gold was found in Alder Gulch, where the Virginia City ghost town now stands.

Modern cattle drives provide the opportunity to relive Montana's frontier past.

Notable People

The history of the state of Montana has been short, relative to the longer history of the United States. Yet Montana has been the birthplace or adopted home of many Americans who have made their mark on the national historical record. Many Montanans have made scientific advances, created important businesses, and served honorably in the military and in public life.

BURTON K. WHEELER
(1822–1975)

Burton K. Wheeler's first political election took him to the Montana House of Representatives in 1910, where he was a champion of labor. From 1913 to 1918, he served as the U.S. district attorney for the state. After an unsuccessful bid for governor, he became a U.S. senator, serving from 1923 to 1947. After public life, he returned to the practice of law.

THOMAS J. WALSH
(1859–1933)

Born on a train bound from Florida to Washington, Thomas J. Walsh was a lawyer elected to the U.S. Senate from Montana in 1912. During a 20-year Senate career, he dedicated himself to issues including child labor laws and gaining the right to vote for women. He is credited with exposing the Teapot Dome corruption scandal during the presidency of Warren G. Harding. In 1933 he was named U.S. attorney general, but he died before taking office.

JEANNETTE RANKIN (1880–1973)

Jeannette Rankin was born near Missoula. In 1910, she became involved in the **suffrage** movement for women. In 1916, she was the first woman elected to the U.S. Congress, sent by Montana to the House of Representatives. She served another term in the House in the early 1940s. Rankin often spoke against war. In 1968, she led a huge protest march against the Vietnam War.

MIKE MANSFIELD (1903–2001)

Democrat Mike Mansfield served in the U.S. Navy, the U.S. Army, and the Marine Corps. In 1942 he was elected to the U.S. House of Representatives. In 1952, he was elected to the U.S. Senate. He was the longest-serving majority leader in the history of the U.S. Senate. In 1977, he became the U.S. ambassador to Japan, and he served in that post until his retirement in 1988.

BRIAN SCHWEITZER (1955–)

Brian Schweitzer was raised on a cattle ranch in Montana. After serving in the U.S. Department of Agriculture, he ran for a U.S. Senate seat in 2000 but was defeated. In 2004, he was elected governor of Montana, and he easily won reelection in 2008.

I DIDN'T KNOW THAT!

Harold C. Urey (1893–1981) started his career as a schoolteacher in Indiana and Montana. He studied chemistry at the University of Montana, going on to win a Nobel Prize in 1934 for discovering a form of hydrogen called deuterium.

Lester C. Thurow (1938–) was born in Livingston. He was dean of the Massachusetts Institute of Technology Sloan School of Management from 1987 to 1993 and has been a professor of economics and management since 1968. He has worked on editorial boards for *The New York Times*, *Newsweek*, and *Time*.

Population

Although Montana is the fourth-largest state in terms of size, its population is relatively small. As of 2010, the state ranked 44th in population.

The largest city in Montana is Billings, with approximately 106,000 inhabitants. Only Billings has more than 100,000 people. Missoula has about 69,000 inhabitants, and Great Falls has about 59,000. The state's **metropolitan** areas are relatively few.

Western and southern Montana are the most populous parts of the state. About half of Montanans live in urban areas, and the other half live in rural areas.

Montana Population 1950–2010

Montana's population has increased in every decade since 1950. What are some of the factors that contribute to a state's population growth?

Number of People

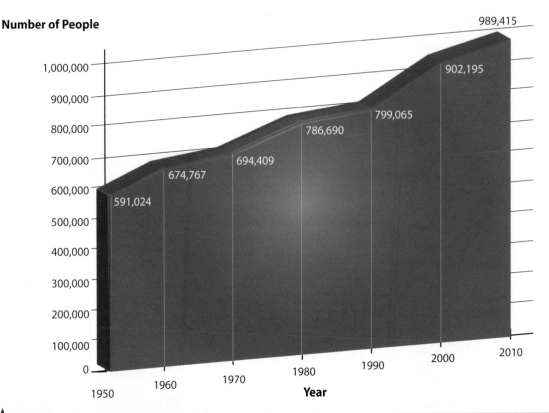

The percentage of American Indians living in Montana is 6.4 percent, much higher than the national average of 1 percent.

In the 2010 Census, Montana's population rank remained at 44th among the 50 states, as it was in 2000, despite a 9.7 percent increase in population.

The discovery of gold and silver was the main reason for Montana's population growth in the 1800s.

Montana has fewer people than Rhode Island does. In total area, though, Montana is 95 times the size of Rhode Island, the smallest state.

In 1900, there were five people per square mile across the state. More than a century later, there are still fewer than seven.

The county courthouse in Great Falls is part of a network of courts. Major cases are handled by 20 district courts. Less serious cases go to municipal courts, police courts, and courts run by a justice of the peace.

Politics and Government

Parts of what is now Montana were, at different times, considered part of the territories of Dakota, Idaho, Louisiana, Missouri, Nebraska, Oregon, and Washington. This was before the Montana Territory was established in 1864.

In 1889 the constitution of the new state of Montana was written. In 1972 the constitution was updated, and it governs the state to this day. The government of Montana, like that of other states, is modeled after the federal government. It has three branches. They are the executive, legislative, and judicial branches.

In the executive branch are the governor, the lieutenant governor, the secretary of state, and the attorney general. All of these officials serve four-year terms. Montana's legislature has 50 senators and 100 representatives. Senators serve four-year terms, and representatives serve two-year terms. The state's courts are headed by a Supreme Court with seven justices. Each justice is elected to an eight-year term.

The Montana state song is called "Montana."

Here is an excerpt from the song:

Tell me of that Treasure State
Story always new,
Tell of its beauties grand
And its hearts so true.
Mountains of sunset fire
The land I love the best
Let me grasp the hand of one
From out the golden West
Montana, Montana,
Glory of the West

Of all the states from coast
*   to coast,*
You're easily the best.
Montana, Montana,
Where skies are always blue
M-O-N-T-A-N-A,
Montana, I love you.

Montana is one of only five states in which the state government does not charge a general sales tax.

Cultural Groups

Many immigrants went to western Montana to work in the silver and copper mines in the 1800s. Soon after, more newcomers made their way to the eastern plains to claim the huge amount of land that was available for farming. At the time, Montana had too few people for the amount of work available, and Europe was facing the opposite problem. People traveled to the new state from Ireland, Germany, Poland, and Italy to earn a living and to begin a new life. Different ethnic groups settled in Montana and began their own communities. By 1910 one-fourth of Montana's residents were from countries other than the United States.

Hutterite women wear scarves on their heads and long skirts. The men dress in dark trousers and wear dark hats.

Montana powwows attract American Indians from throughout the state and beyond. Dancers compete in events such as the jingle dance and grass dance.

Several religious groups **migrated** to Montana in order to practice their beliefs in peace. Mennonite settlers were among them, though many Mennonites left when the state government made speaking German illegal during World War II. Mormons, also known as members of the Church of Jesus Christ of Latter-day Saints, also settled in Montana. There are now more than 45,000 members of the Mormon church in the state. In addition, there are a number of Hutterite communities in Montana. Hutterites believe strongly in living simple, nonviolent lives. They live in rural areas and avoid much of modern society. Farming is an important economic activity within Hutterite communities, and the Hutterites sell their goods in nearby cities or towns.

Although they were once Montana's sole residents, American Indians now make up only about 6 percent of Montana's population. Many live on reservations. Reservations uphold long-standing traditions. They also provide opportunities for education and training.

Arts and Entertainment

The calendar is filled with arts and entertainment events in Montana. In February, the Big Sky Documentary Film Festival in Missoula showcases nonfiction film. Living history weekends are held all summer at the Outdoor Living History Museum in Nevada City, which has one of the biggest collections of Western items outside of the Smithsonian. Bozeman holds the Sweet Pea Festival in August, a celebration of the arts that includes dance workshops and art exhibits and sales. In September, the Running of the Sheep through Main Street in Reed Point is part of a sheep-themed day that ends with a street dance, complete with live bands.

Artists of all kinds have called Montana home. Young Charlie Russell had two passions. He wanted to be a cowboy and to draw wildlife. When he was 16 years old, his father sent him to Montana, and his dreams became reality. Russell's artistic career began in 1887. He illustrated a terrible winter in Montana by drawing a starved, frozen cow surrounded by wolves. This famous work of art is known as *Waiting for a Chinook*. Russell took an interest in American Indians and their culture, painting them in detail. He is considered to be one of the greatest painters and sculptors of the early West.

Dana Carvey was born in Missoula. The comedian became famous on the TV show Saturday Night Live. *He is known for characters such as "Garth" and for his impressions of politicians and entertainers, such as Regis Philbin.*

Montana has also raised or attracted many entertainers. Comedian Dana Carvey was born in Missoula. Actress Michelle Williams is from Kalispell. Montana-born Evel Knievel has earned the reputation as the greatest motorcycle daredevil in the world. In 1966 Knievel began his career as a stuntman. He performed dangerous motorcycle jumps, flying off ramps and sailing over objects. Knievel jumped over as many as 50 cars at one time.

Evel Knievel's son, Robbie, performs motorcycle stunts for today's audiences. Just like his father, Robbie delights and shocks fans with his amazing antics.

Constructed in the 1990s with the help of more than 200 volunteers, the Missoula carousel was the first fully hand-carved U.S. carousel built since the 1930s. Each horse honors a local resident or is based on American Indian culture.

A. B. Guthrie, Jr., grew up in Montana. His Pulitzer Prize–winning novel, *The Way West*, depicts the settlement of the Northwest. He also wrote the screenplay for the classic Western movie *Shane*.

The rhythm and blues pianist George Winston grew up in Miles City. His 1999 recording, *Plains*, celebrates the region.

Jeff Ament, who plays bass for the alternative rock group Pearl Jam, grew up in Big Sandy, where his father served as mayor. Ament is known for his mastery of 12-string and fretless bass guitars.

Sports

Fly fishing is a popular outdoor sport in Montana. The book and movie *A River Runs Through It* depict the rivers near Missoula as a fisher's paradise. Norman Maclean, the author, wrote of his trips to the Clark Fork River with his father and brother. In Montana, fishers of all levels of ability can be seen practicing their fly casting in open areas. During fishing season, people from all over the country head to Montana's rivers and streams.

As a Rocky Mountain state with snowy winters, Montana is also a haven for winter sports enthusiasts. Some of those sports are extreme, such as blade running. Professional skydivers jump out of a helicopter over a ski hill. A parachute keeps them in the air while they wind through a course of 10-foot-tall banners, called blades. Ice sailing and ice surfing are for those who enjoy speed. On special boats, winter sailors are propelled by the wind across frozen lakes. Ice surfers attach blades to their shoes and cling to a sail that fills with wind as they "surf" across the ice. Others enjoy the thrill of ice climbing.

Ice climbing spots are rated on the Water Ice, or WI, system. There is a scale from WI 1, an easy walk, to WI 6, which means there is overhanging ice and very little protection for the climber.

The University of Montana Grizzlies football team has won multiple Big Sky Conference titles and National Collegiate Athletic Association championships.

The state boasts many downhill ski areas. Because Montana is a large state with a small population, the lines for the ski lifts are rarely long. Snowboarders are also welcome. Many of the state's ski resorts offer remarkable snowboard parks, featuring halfpipes, board jumps, and banked turns.

For team sports, there are two main universities fielding teams that delight Montana fans. Signs of support are plastered throughout Missoula, home of the University of Montana Grizzlies. The scene is similar in Bozeman, hometown of the Montana State University Bobcats. Along with the schools' students, Bozeman and Missoula residents come out to watch basketball, football, and volleyball.

Race to the Sky is a 350-mile dogsled race commemorating the training of sled dogs in Montana in the early 1940s for use during World War II.

The first Wild Horse Stampede was held at the turn of the 20th century. Today this three-day Montana rodeo features a competition in which people saddle up and ride wild horses.

An annual American Legion rodeo held east of Helena is called the Wildest One Day Show on Earth.

World-class ice climbers go to the Bozeman area for challenging climbs. Ice climbing is growing in popularity in the state.

Hiking and camping are popular summer pastimes in Montana's mountains. Most of the federally owned land is available for camping.

MetraPark, in Billings, is a large "events campus" that includes an arena used for both horse racing and motor sports.

National Averages Comparison

T he United States is a federal republic, consisting of fifty states and the District of Columbia. Alaska and Hawai'i are the only non-contiguous, or non-touching, states in the nation. Today, the United States of America is the third-largest country in the world in population. The United States Census Bureau takes a census, or count of all the people, every ten years. It also regularly collects other kinds of data about the population and the economy. How does Montana compare to the national average?

Comparison Chart

United States 2010 Census Data *	USA	Montana
Admission to Union	NA	November 8, 1889
Land Area (in square miles)	3,537,438.44	145,552.43
Population Total	308,745,538	989,415
Population Density (people per square mile)	87.28	6.79
Population Percentage Change (April 1, 2000, to April 1, 2010)	9.7%	9.7%
White Persons (percent)	72.4%	82.8%
Black Persons (percent)	12.6%	11.6%
American Indian and Alaska Native Persons (percent)	0.9%	0.5%
Asian Persons (percent)	4.8%	1.6%
Native Hawaiian and Other Pacific Islander Persons (percent)	0.2%	0.1%
Some Other Race (percent)	6.2%	1.3%
Persons Reporting Two or More Races (percent)	2.9%	2.1%
Persons of Hispanic or Latino Origin (percent)	16.3%	3.5%
Not of Hispanic or Latino Origin (percent)	83.7%	96.5%
Median Household Income	$52,029	$43,948
Percentage of People Age 25 or Over Who Have Graduated from High School	80.4%	87.2%

*All figures are based on the 2010 United States Census, with the exception of the last two items.

How to Improve My Community

Strong communities make strong states. Think about what features are important in your community. What do you value? Education? Health? Forests? Safety? Beautiful spaces? Government works to help citizens create ideal living conditions that are fair to all by providing services in communities. Consider what changes you could make in your community. How would they improve your state as a whole? Using this concept web as a guide, write a report that outlines the features you think are most important in your community and what improvements could be made. A strong state needs strong communities.

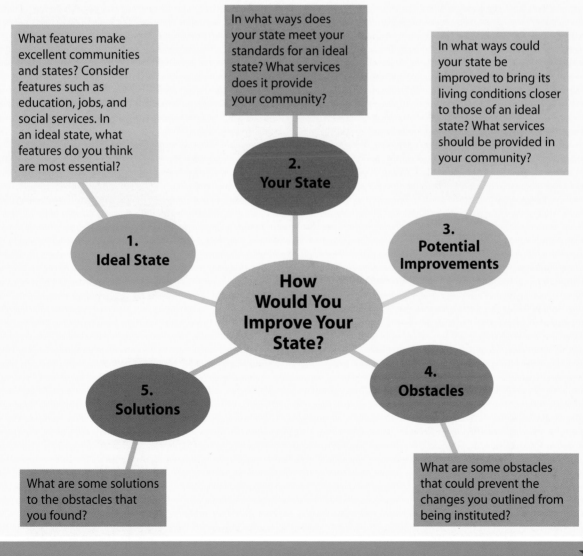

What features make excellent communities and states? Consider features such as education, jobs, and social services. In an ideal state, what features do you think are most essential?

In what ways does your state meet your standards for an ideal state? What services does it provide your community?

In what ways could your state be improved to bring its living conditions closer to those of an ideal state? What services should be provided in your community?

2.
Your State

1.
Ideal State

3.
Potential
Improvements

How
Would You
Improve Your
State?

5.
Solutions

4.
Obstacles

What are some solutions to the obstacles that you found?

What are some obstacles that could prevent the changes you outlined from being instituted?

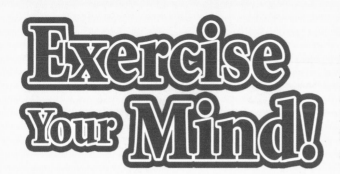

Exercise Your Mind!

Think about these questions and then use your research skills to find the answers and learn more fascinating facts about Montana. A teacher, librarian, or parent may be able to help you locate the best sources to use in your research.

1 What is Triple Divide Peak?

2 What is the world's oldest national park?

3 True or False: Lewis and Clark visited the caverns that bear their name.

4 What event occurred in Loma, Montana, on January 15, 1972?

5 There are many bears in Montana. What should you do if you bump into one?

6 From December 1995 to May 1999 what speed limit was posted on Montana's major highways?

7 What happened to Montana's Grinnel Glacier in 1980?

8 How did the Montana town of Ekalaka earn the nickname Skeleton Flats?

Words to Know

capitol: the building that houses the legislature

chinook: a warm wind that blows from the mountains

distinguish: identify one kind from another

environmentalists: people who protect and care for the environment

expedition: a journey made for exploration

extinction: when a species no longer exists

extraction: the act of obtaining something through a chemical, physical, or mechanical process

metropolitan: referring to a large urban area, usually a city and surrounding suburbs

migrated: moved to a new place

moccasins: shoes made entirely of soft leather, first worn by American Indians

necessities: requirements for life, such as food, clothing, and shelter

powwows: American Indian ceremonies or councils

reintroduced: brought into an area after an absence

reservations: lands reserved for American Indians

suffrage: right to vote in elections

Superfund: a U.S. Environmental Protection Agency fund that aids cleanup of environmentally unsafe or toxic areas

Index

Log on to www.av2books.com

AV² by Weigl brings you media enhanced books that support active learning. Go to www.av2books.com, and enter the special code found on page 2 of this book. You will gain access to enriched and enhanced content that supplements and complements this book. Content includes video, audio, web links, quizzes, a slide show, and activities.

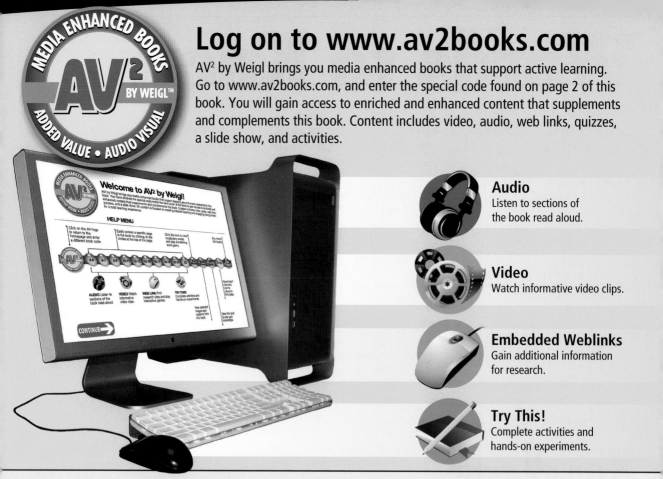

Audio
Listen to sections of the book read aloud.

Video
Watch informative video clips.

Embedded Weblinks
Gain additional information for research.

Try This!
Complete activities and hands-on experiments.

WHAT'S ONLINE?

Try This!	Embedded Weblinks	Video	EXTRA FEATURES
Test your knowledge of the state in a mapping activity.	Discover more attractions in Montana.	Watch a video introduction to Montana.	**Audio** Listen to sections of the book read aloud.
Find out more about precipitation in your city.	Learn more about the history of the state.	Watch a video about the features of the state.	**Key Words** Study vocabulary, and complete a matching word activity.
Plan what attractions you would like to visit in the state.	Learn the full lyrics of the state song.		**Slide Show** View images and captions, and prepare a presentation.
Learn more about the early natural resources of the state.			**Quizzes** Test your knowledge.
Write a biography about a notable resident of Montana.			
Complete an educational census activity.			

AV² was built to bridge the gap between print and digital. We encourage you to tell us what you like and what you want to see in the future.

Sign up to be an AV² Ambassador at www.av2books.com/ambassador.